friendship

A HIGHLY FAVOURED LIFE DEVOTIONAL

Table of Contents

Dedication

To those faithful ladies who have known the hurt or lose of a friend, thank you for never quitting but for teaching us by example how to build godly friendships.

Introduction

Come on, ladies. We all enjoy a good shopping day with a friend. We may stop for coffee for a quick pick-me-up. We shop at our favorite shops, then grab a salad (or burger and fries) for lunch. There is constant chatter the whole time. We ask each other's opinion on the shirt we pull off the rack. We take the time to research what department store is running a sale, maybe opting to swing by the thrift store instead because all red tag items are 50% off! Then, we chat some more.

We take the time to share our favorite activity from the week. We mention the upcoming events in our lives. We share life struggles and wins. We try to encourage and relate with one another. At the end of the outing, we go home with sore feet and tongues and maybe even bank accounts, but we already have the next outing and "chat session" in the books for next month.

Okay, maybe it doesn't always look quite like that, but you get the idea. God gave us the ability to build friendships. He gave us the privilege to be a friend to others too. But Christ set the example of a perfect Friend. He expects us to model our friendships after His. What an amazing, overwhelming responsibility!

Spending time with friends should bring us joy and encouragement in our daily walk with the Lord. We should strive to center our friendships on Christ and His Word. We should desire to find friends that are willing to grow with us in their spiritual walk with the Lord. This ensures that we can grow together, keeping each other accountable.

Before beginning this first devotional, ask yourself these three questions.

- What kind of Friend is Christ to me?
- What kind of friend am I to others?
- What kind of friends do I surround myself with?

A Friend Indeed

By Susan Hutchens

O magnify the LORD with me, and let us exalt his name together.

Psalm 34:3

Everything's better with a friend, right? Shopping, coffee, lunch . . . you name it, we women love to do things with our friends. David wrote in Psalm 34, "Magnify the Lord with me, and let us exalt his name together." That sounds nice and cozy, like something we would do at a ladies' retreat or fellowship meeting where life is generally good, and we are happy to be there. But where was David when he wrote this psalm? Let's take a closer look.

When this psalm was written, David was hiding in a cave because King Saul wanted him dead. He had run to Achish, king of Gath (remember Goliath?) because King Saul was trying to kill him. But Achish was a little suspicious of David, the hero and future king of Israel. So, David thought it best to act like he had gone crazy. He scrabbled on the town gates and drooled in his beard. Achish wasn't buying it. So David had to run again. He took refuge in the cave of

After you hear the problem, help her look to the Lord.

Adullam near Gath. It wasn't long before four hundred other men had joined him. These guys were the cream of the crop: in distress, in debt, and discontented. What a mess!

Four hundred and one men in a cave hiding from death, stress, creditors, bitterness – life in general. So David stands up and says, "Magnify the Lord with me, and let us exalt his name together!" What? Praise the Lord when my life is a mess, and I'm on the run? We have an important lesson here. Four hundred men had come to David looking for a leader, someone who could help them out of the mess they were in. They probably expected him to lead them into battles, have lots of adventures, live a little dangerously, and have some fun along the way. Kind of like we do when we confide in our friends. We want a little sympathy, maybe a good cry, and some indignation that life is treating us so bad at the moment. We want to fight, and who better to help us fight than our besties?

So what's a bestie to do? Turn her friend to Jesus. If we follow David's example, we turn her around and point to Jesus. Magnify Him. Exalt Him. Don't ignore the problem or minimize her distress. I'm not saying that! But after you hear the problem, help her look to the Lord!

Imagine what would happen if, the next time a friend came to you in distress, you magnified the Lord with her! You'd encourage her to trust Him (Proverbs 3:5). You'd point out the good things that are happening in the midst of the bad (Philippians 4:8). You'd encourage biblical decisions rather than worldly ones (II Peter 1:3). You'd draw her higher, rather than sinking to the depths with her (Hebrews 10:24). You'd discourage sinning with her words (Job 2:10). And you'd help her to find joy in the midst of her troubles, because God inhabits the praises of His people (Psalm 22:3), and in His presence is fullness of joy (Psalm 16:11).

The next time you have a friend in need, really be there for her. Don't just listen to her and try to help her in whatever situation she faces, but also encourage her to "magnify the Lord with me, and let us exalt his name together."

friendship

Notes

Prayers

A Desire for Right Friends

By Brianna Hewitt

Iron sharpeneth iron; so a man sharpeneth the countenance of his friend.

Proverbs 27:17

There have probably been times in most of our lives when we feel as though we don't have very many friends, especially the right kind of friends God would want us to have. God not only gives us warnings about who we should consider as a friend, but also the type of friend we should strive to be. Let's look at the scriptures and see what God says about friendships.

First of all, God is our Friend. Proverbs 18:24 says, "A man that hath friends must shew himself friendly: and there is a friend that sticketh closer than a brother."

Secondly, a good friend is there to help and not hurt. Ecclesiastes 4:10 says, "For if they fall, the one will lift up his fellow: but woe to him that is alone when he falleth; for he hath not another to help him up." When times of heartache and trials come into our lives, it is assuring to know we can always go to God. But good friends will also be there praying for me in those difficult times. God says in

Galatians 6:2, "Bear ye one another's burdens, and so fulfill the law of Christ." Are we the friends who lift up a brother or sister in prayer when they are struggling? Do our "friends" care about others or just themselves? Be mindful of those who we allow ourselves to get close to because they will influence us and not always in the right way.

Lastly, the right friend will be an encourager. Thank God for the friends we have that keep us pointed in the right direction. Philippians 1:3-5 says, "I thank my God upon every remembrance of you, Always in every prayer of mine for you all making request with joy, For your fellowship in the gospel from the first day until now." Do the friends you have sharpen you to be a better, Christian? If not, take a step back and ask the Lord to help you in the area of friendship. If you desire to have the right friends and are following the Lord, He will give you what you desire. Psalms 37:4 "Delight thyself also in the Lord; and he shall give thee the desires of thine heart."

Good friends will also be there praying for me in those difficult times.

friendship

Notes

Prayers

A Faithful Friend

By Victoria Kiker

Faithful are the wounds of a friend; but the kisses of an enemy are deceitful.

Proverbs 27:6

The book of Proverbs is replete with counsel regarding the subject of friendship. Biblical friendship is one of the most treasured gifts that God has given us here on earth. Yet, many of us struggle with finding friends who will be lifelong companions. As women, we deal with insecurities within ourselves, and the hope of finding a friend or two who will accept us as we are seems daunting. Let me say, I understand! I have been blessed to have a few faithful friends.

Please understand, when I say a few, I mean very few. I have many dear acquaintances, but I could probably count on one hand the number of close friends I hold in high regard. However, I believe I'm in good company. The Lord Jesus chose only twelve men to walk with Him through His ministry on earth; three were included in His inner circle and only one - "whom Jesus loved" - leaned on His bosom at the Last Supper (John 13:23). Judas Iscariot was also included in the twelve. Remember his kiss of betrayal in the garden? This

"If I take offense easily; if I am content to continue in cold unfriendliness, though friendship be possible, then I know nothing of Calvary's love."

- Amy Carmichael

alone should prove that not all friendships are equal and betrayal is a true possibility in any of our relationships. Through His sovereign foreknowledge, Jesus knew of the imminent betrayal, yet He still chose to be a friend. We should follow Christ's example of earnest friendship, allowing Him to guide our relationships.

My friends and I have made a covenant to be the friend of Proverbs 27:6. We have promised that when one of us is faltering spiritually, whether that be within our homes, with our spouses or children, or in our Biblical stands of holy living and Christ-honoring convictions, we will call each other out on those transgressions. This is not to intentionally bring pain to one another's lives. On the contrary, we deeply love and care for one another (Proverbs 17:17). In order to love well, you must give truth and accept truth from your friendships. This outlook may seem contradictory. You may believe a true friend would never wound you. But a true, faithful friend will speak truth in your life even though it may hurt at the moment.

The best example of a faithful friend is found in our Lord. If you are in pursuit of a close walk with Him, He is not going to allow you to continually sin and do wrong without conviction or consequences. As a Friend, He wants what's best for you! The wounds of His friendship are there for your benefit, not your destruction. Proverbs 17:17, "Iron sharpeneth iron; so a man sharpeneth the countenance of his friend." Until iron has been sharpened and made useful, there is no value. I need friends who will keep me sharp spiritually so that

I may be effective for the kingdom of God. My sharpening may be provoking and even painful at times. Nevertheless, I need to learn to appreciate the encouragement as well as the candid criticisms from my faithful friends.

What kind of friend are you? Do you speak biblical truth when a friend is faltering? Do you look out for the spiritual well-being of your companions? More importantly, will you gratefully accept the truth that may wound you? Amy Carmichael said, "If I take offense easily; if I am content to continue in cold unfriendliness, though friendship be possible, then I know nothing of Calvary's love." My prayer for you, dear reader, is that you find friendship. First and foremost with our Savior, for He is the dearest Friend one could ever find, then with a few faithful friends who will walk along with you in this journey of life.

"God, send me a friend that will tell me of my faults." - Thomas Fuller

friendship

Notes

Prayers

My Best Friend

By Debra Birner

His mouth is most sweet: yea, he is altogether lovely.
This is my beloved, and this is my friend, O daughters of Jerusalem.

Song of Solomon 5:16

Ahhh, the Shulamite woman is adoring her Shepherd, her beloved. What does she say? "This is my beloved, and this is my friend..." Let me tell you about my friend. I have a friend with whom I love to spend all of my time. If I want to go shopping, I ask my friend to come along. If I want to chat about what's going on in my life, I call my friend, unless we can be together – which is much better than a phone call! My friend has known me for a long time and enjoys being with me as much as I enjoy being with my friend.

If you haven't guessed yet, my friend is my spouse, my husband, my true, constant companion. Yes, I have other "friends," but my relationship with them pales in comparison to the friendship I have with my husband. I have had many friends that have come and gone through different seasons in my life – some that I thought would always be in my life. But my husband has been my friend and my spouse since I was a teenager.

From time to time a friend of mine may ask if I want to spend time with her and have a ladies night or a shopping spree or whatever. While there is nothing wrong with those activities, if my husband is available to be with me, I generally choose instead to spend time with him. Over the years of managing jobs and raising children, we have found that when we can be together, that has always been more of a blessing to us than to have separate activities. Yes, there are always times when we are apart and with other people, but whenever possible, we have chosen to be together. If another friend of mine wishes to get together for an evening, I encourage her to come to my home and have dinner with my husband and I or do an activity with us, so we can all enjoy the fellowship together.. Likewise, when we choose ministries to become a part of, we try to choose things we can do together. Being together brings us great joy, no matter what activity we are participating in during that time.

I recognize that I live in a way that is different from many in this regard. However, in a time when many marriages end in divorce, I feel safe and secure in my marriage, praising the Lord that He has given me such a tremendous gift. And yes, Jesus Christ is my Friend that sticketh closer than a brother (or a spouse!). But I believe He gave us marriage so that we can have an earthly picture of what a Friend the Lord Jesus is to us.

friendship

Notes

Prayers

Friend or Enemy?

By Kelly Byrley

Ye adulterers and adulteresses, know ye not that the friendship of the world is enmity with God? whosoever therefore will be a friend of the world is the enemy of God.

James 4:4

At first, we may skip over this verse thinking it couldn't possibly apply to us. Of course, we are not God's enemy! Of course, we are not a friend of the world because one of the definitions of the word friend is, "an attendant; a companion." That doesn't describe us. We are saved. We don't cozy up to the world. We try our best to do right and to live right. We don't rebel against God. We try to be obedient and follow His prompting. But are there other ways that God could still consider us a friend of the world? Let's keep in mind that things don't necessarily have to be wrong to still be considered "of the world." Let me explain what I mean by that.

One of the definitions of friend is "one who is attached to another by affection." We can ask ourselves some simple questions to determine whether or not we could be attached to something of the world. Could I give to faith promise missions if I just didn't

.....whosoever therefore will be a friend of the world is the enemy of God.

- James 4:4

spend so much money on _____ every month? Do I make time to keep up on social media, but fail to keep up on my prayer life? Do I commit to other regularly scheduled events, but soul-winning is not one of them? Do I slack in serving my family or in my outside ministries because I could use some extra sleep, me-time, etc? What we spend our time and money on is what we are attached to. It's what our heart desires. Sometimes, if we are honest with ourselves, our hearts desire the things of the world more than the things of the Lord. Those things may not even be sinful things, but they become sinful when they get out of place in our list of priorities.

Another definition of the word friend is "one not hostile." So by this definition, we must be an actual enemy of the world to avoid being considered a friend of the world. It seems pretty simple at first, but we must ask ourselves if we are truly enemies of the world. One of the definitions of enemy is "the opposing force in war." We are all aware that we are in a spiritual battle, but do we go on the offense in that battle or do we only spring into action defensively when we are under attack? Are we not only pushing back on the agendas that the world is trying to force us to accept but are we also sharing the gospel more and more?

Another definition of enemy is "an adversary; one who hates or dislikes." Do we live like Jude 1:23 describes, "And others save with fear, pulling them out of the fire; hating even the garment spotted by the flesh." Do we hate sin so much that we are actively looking for ways to destroy even the slightest bit of it before it has a chance to spot our garments? Are we so aggressive in our soul-winning efforts that we could be described as pulling people from the fire?

This was extremely convicting for me to write because I realized that, at times, God must have considered me His enemy. If this could be said about you as well, don't despair! We can rest in the assurance of what Psalm 145:8 says, "The LORD is gracious, and full of compassion; slow to anger, and of great mercy." All we have to do is ask Him for forgiveness and strive to change these things in our lives so that when the Lord thinks of us, He will not consider us His enemy.

friendship

Notes

Prayers

A Lifetime Friend

By Andrea Leeder

And the scripture was fulfilled which saith, Abraham believed God, and it was imputed unto him for righteousness: and he was called the Friend of God.

James 2:23

Wouldn't it be wonderful to have God call you His friend? Abraham was called the friend of God. A friendship takes time to cultivate. You don't just talk to someone once or twice, and all of a sudden, you are best friends. You must spend quality time with them, and get to know them on a personal level. You learn about their likes and dislikes. You work at your relationship with acts of service that show them you care.

How is your friendship with the Lord? Have you learned His likes and dislikes? Do you serve Him as you should? Could you say that you have a friendship with the Lord? Or is it possible that you have a friendship with the world?

The Bible tells us in James 4:4, "Ye adulterers and adulteresses, know ye not that the friendship of the world is enmity with God? whosoever therefore will be a friend of the world is the enemy of God." When we allow worldly things to creep into our lives, we are pushing our friendship with God aside. When we choose to live for ourselves and seek the pleasures of this world, we become God's enemy.

Faithfully reading God's Word, attending church every time the doors are open, praying, soulwinning, serving, and encouraging others are all ways we can cultivate our friendship with God. Learning what is pleasing to Him, talking to Him, and doing what His will is for your life will create a friendship with God.

John 15:14, "Ye are my friends, if ye do whatsoever I command you." God is the best Friend you could ever have! It would be foolish, Christian, not to take the steps necessary to make God our best Friend. He will never leave us nor forsake us. We can rely on Him in the darkest times. We can talk to Him any time about everything. He understands our weaknesses and knows us better than anyone else. He can encourage us as no one else can. He gives us blessings like no one else does.

If your friendship with the Lord is sweet and you can be called a friend of God, enjoy the blessings that His friendship brings and keep serving Him! Have you strayed away from the Lord? Are there some things that you could do to make your friendship sweeter with the Lord? If so, I challenge you to become a friend of God and have a closer relationship with Him.

Psalm 68:19, "Blessed be the Lord, who daily loadeth us with benefits, even the God of our salvation. Selah."

friendship

Notes

Prayers

Friend of Sinners

By Tresa Barber

Be not afraid of their faces, for I am with thee to deliver thee, saith the LORD.

Jeremiah 1:8

Jesus is a friend to sinners. We see His example of friendship all through Scripture. We each have a circle of influence where God has placed us, and this is where He wants to use us to accomplish His purposes.

Friendship ultimately creates pportunities to share the gospel with our neighbors, coworkers, and acquaintances. As Christians, we will often need to make the first move in friendship. Proverbs 18:24 says, "A man that hath friends must show himself friendly."

One day, our youngest son was playing on a dirt pile next door that belonged to our neighbor. After a while, the neighbor came out and told us angrily that we should stay off the dirt hill. I was mortified, but I knew that he had a right to ask my child to leave. I apologized, and a few days later, my husband and I visited them with some homemade brownies. We had a nice chat and began a friendly relationship. Some months later, we had the opportunity to lead the

39

couple to Christ. I'm glad that God gave me the grace to apologize about the dirt hill and to reach out in kindness to them!

We moved to a new neighborhood three years ago. Living on a corner lot has allowed us to meet many neighbors as they walk by while we are out working in the yard. Covid happened when we had been here only six months, and not as many people went outside or stopped to talk. The Lord put it on my heart one day to go across the street and speak to a couple whom I had not seen for months. The man answered the door, but he was stern and barely civil while I tried to make small talk and asked how they were doing. When I left, I felt it had gone badly, but to my surprise, they soon asked me to do them a favor, which I did, and we exchanged phone numbers. The lady now calls me from time to time, and we have a nice chat. I am reminded of Jeremiah 1:8 which says to "Be not afraid of their faces: for I am with thee to deliver thee, saith the LORD." I'm glad I visited them. I am hoping to have a Bible study in my home and invite my neighbor and some other ladies to come!

Both examples I have shared contain negative aspects. But these are things that happen as we interact with people, and we can pray that God will work in people's hearts in spite of things that we see as obstacles. My prayer is that God would help me to see more opportunities to show myself friendly, so that I might share the love of Christ!

friendship

Notes

Prayers

Friendship "Guilt Train"

By Alicia Moss

To every thing there is a season,
and a time to every purpose under the heaven:

Ecclesiates 3:1

I am the guilty woman who is always riding the "guilt train." If only I could be better... If only I had more time...If only... One of those "if only" statements quite often ends with "I wish I were a better friend." I have been blessed with many Christian and non-Christian friends in my life. One definition I read defining a friend was "a person on the same side in a struggle." In the secular world, I have had many friends who have helped me carry the challenges of being a college student, teaching students steeped in poverty, and cheering me on to be a top public school teacher in my county. I have also had many Christian friends who have encouraged me to stand for the Lord, be strong in my convictions, and learn more from His Word. But I continued to ride the "guilt train" of not being a good friend until I began to dig into His Word.

When I looked intoGod's Word, I remembered my purpose. Genesis 2:18, "...It is not good that the man should be alone; I will make him an help meet for him." He could have created a male best friend for Adam that would want to hunt, fish, shoot hoops, or drive some nails. But God did not create a male best friend. As we know, God created Eve to be Adam's "BFF." I must remember my purpose and if my "Adam" is not my best friend, then I am wrong and need to get my friendships in the right priority.

Then, I was led to my favorite chapter in the Bible... Proverbs 31. (I hope you heard my sarcasm. I honestly don't like her most of the time.) Take a moment and read that chapter through the lens of friendship. I don't see a time when she took the time to meet up at Starbucks or took a day trip to go shopping. Are those things wrong? No! But if all I'm doing is meeting up with my girlfriends to socialize, I must get my friendships in the right priority. I have a husband to be a help meet to and must strive to "...do him good..." Proverbs 31:12. I have been given children to train in the nurture and admonition of the Lord. I must study God's Word so that I can be wise — "she openeth her mouth with wisdom...," Proverbs 31:26. While fellowshipping with friends, am I just "chewing the fat" or are our conversations profitable?

I hope you are determined not to ride the guilt train of not being a "good friend." God has different seasons of life for each of His children. Your season may be steeped in schoolwork. Your season may be finding God's will for your life. You may be in the season of barely surviving through nightly feedings or teaching your kids to read. Friendships matter, but God wants our priorities to be right even in our friendships. Don't ride the guilt train of "I'm not a good friend." Friends give each other grace. And remember, a true friend will always be, no matter the season.

44

friendship

Notes

Prayers

Nurturing your Friendship with your Best Friend for Life

By Anja Meyer

*And the Lord God said, It is not good that the man should be alone;
I will make him an help meet for him.*

Genesis 2:18

I cannot really remember the first time I met my best friend for life. He assures me it was just before our first lecture at the university. He remembers the location and even what I wore. I do, however, remember the exact moment I started to take notice of this young man. It was at a Friday evening youth gathering at our pastor's house. After hearing this boy's answer to a tricky question, Pastor exclaimed, "This is a young man after my own heart!" I remember thinking, "Hmm!!" The LORD has been so good to us, and we were able to celebrate our sixteenth wedding anniversary this year.

When thinking about friendships, the friendship with our husband should be the most important to and the most treasured by each of us. This is a friendship that should outlive all other

The friendship
with our husband
should be the most
important to and the
most treasured by
each of us.

friendships, and since we spend by far the most time with this best friend of ours, there are plenty of opportunities to build into and nurture this friendship. Let us look at truths about friendship from the Word of God.

1. This marriage-friendship was created by God as a special blessing. Appreciate and enjoy it! Genesis 2:18, "And the Lord God said, It is not good that the man should be alone; I will make him an help meet for him." Proverbs 18:22, "Whoso findeth a wife findeth a good thing, and obtaineth favour of the Lord."

2. In the day-to-day "mundaness" of life, we may forget the specialness of this friendship. Make an extra effort to make eye contact during the day, smile at him often, and speak in a pleasant tone of voice. Little things make all the difference! Proverbs 18:24, "A man that hath friends must shew himself friendly: and there is a friend that sticketh closer than a brother."

3. Spend time together! Find out about his likes and dislikes, admire him for his hobbies, and make time for plenty of conversation. You will find that you grow more and more alike, enjoying the same kind of things. Proverbs 27:17, "Iron sharpeneth iron; so a man sharpeneth the countenance of his friend."

4. Remember that none of us are perfect; we are all human. Your best friend may not always be kind or selfless. There will be plenty of opportunities for you to get mad or upset, but the LORD has a better way. Proverbs 17:17, "A friend loveth at all times, and a brother is born for adversity." Luke 17:4, "And if he trespass against thee seven times in a day, and seven times in a day turn again to thee, saying, I repent; thou shalt forgive him."

There is so much more to be said about this friendship we share with our husbands, but I hope and pray that these verses will encourage you on this journey with your best friend.

friendship

Notes

Prayers

Friendships: God's Special Blessings

By Rita Nichols

Greater love hath no man than this, that a man lay down his life for his friends.

John 15:13

So many things come to mind when we talk about friendships. The Bible says in Proverbs 18:24, "A man that hath friends must shew himself friendly...." There are several types of friends. First of all, you have a casual friend. This is the person that you say a passing "hello" to in church or on the street. Secondly, you have a good friend. You may spend time together, maybe work together, and do projects together. Thirdly, you have a lifetime friend. These are rare friendships that the Lord brings into our lives.

In my life, I have had many good friendships. The Lord has brought people into my life for a season. The Lord used these people to be a blessing to me and allowed me to be a blessing to them for a time. In Proverbs 27:17 it says, "Iron sharpeneth iron; so a man sharpeneth the countenance of his friend." God placed these special people in my path for a specific time in my life. I am sure that we all can think of friends that were very close at one point and somehow lost contact with them over time.

I am privileged to have friends that have lasted a lifetime. While we may not see each other often or stay in contact, whenever we talk, the pages of time just fall away. We have so many rich memories of laughter and joy. James 5:16 says, "Confess your faults one to another, pray one for another, that ye may be healed. The effectual fervent prayer of a righteous man availeth much." These are the friends that I have cried with, shared burdens with, prayed with, and often served with in the ministry.

Those of us who are married can hopefully think of our spouse as our closest friend. They are our partners and companions. I am very fortunate to have a husband that loves the Lord. I go to him often to seek counsel or just to unburden myself.

John 15:13 says, "Greater love hath no man than this, that a man lay down his life for his friends." The Lord gives us the ultimate example of true friendship. In following His guidance, let us cherish those whom the Lord has placed in our lives.

Remember that our greatest Friend is the Lord Jesus Christ. He loves us in a way that no one else ever could. Psalm 139:1, "O Lord thou hast searched me, and known me." The Lord knows us completely, yet He still loves us.

friendship

Notes

Prayers

Growing Godly Friendships

By Breanna Patton

*The aged women likewise, that they be in behaviour as becometh holiness,
not false accusers, not given to much wine, teachers of good things;
That they may teach the young women to be sober, to love their husbands,
to love their children, To be discreet, chaste, keepers at home, good,
obedient to their own husbands, that the word of God be not blasphemed.*

Titus 2:3-5

Christian lady, have you ever found yourself discouraged because there were no other ladies your age at church activities? Because I know that I have. Recently, the Lord reprimanded me for this discouragement and showed me how great a blessing in disguise it could be. Just read Titus 2:3-5. The Lord is telling us here that it is the job of the older ladies to teach the younger ladies how to live right, in order that God's Word "be not blasphemed."

The aged women in the church are the ones that I, as a younger lady, should get to know. They have gone through more of life than I have, and they have much wisdom for me to glean from. Yes, it is good to have friends of the same age and stage of life as you, but the Lord specifically commands the older women to teach the younger women. These older ladies can give us insight to guide us and keep us from making the same mistakes they made as young wives and mothers.

My pastor's wife said at a recent ladies' Bible study that as a young wife and mother she wished she would have gotten wisdom from some of the older ladies in the church so she could have avoided common mistakes that come with inexperience in these new roles. The Lord has allowed different people to experience different circumstances. Why not learn and grow from someone else's experiences? So today, older lady, find a young lady in your church to mentor and teach. If you are younger, go find a godly older lady and ask them questions and glean from their wisdom.

The aged women in the church are the ones that I, as a younger lady, should get to know.

friendship

Notes

Prayers

Wounds of a Friend

By Elizabeth Garrett

Faithful are the wounds of a friend; but the kisses of an enemy are deceitful.

Proverbs 27:6

Have you ever been wounded by a friend? I do not refer to someone who pretended to be your friend and then turned against you and betrayed you. No, I speak of that friend who you know loves you and wants what is best for you, that person that you can count on any time to be there for you.

Perhaps you were seeking validation for a reaction you had in a situation or for feelings you had toward another person; or you were making decisions and expected that person to support you. Yet, she did not respond as you expected. She disagreed with you or confronted you and therefore, wounded you. She told you what you did not want to hear.

Solomon here, under the inspiration of the Holy Spirit, says that the wounds of a friend are "faithful." That word faithful means "to build up or support; to foster as a parent or nurse; to render firm or faithful." This reminds me of a passage in the New Testament. Paul had written his first epistle to the Corinthian church to correct major problems. He had "wounded" them, so to speak. But note what he says in II Corinthians 7:8-9, "For though I made you sorry with a letter, I do not repent, though I did repent: for I perceive that the same epistle hath made you sorry, though it were but for a season. Now I rejoice, not that ye were made sorry, but that ye sorrowed to repentance: for ye were made sorry after a godly manner, that ye might receive damage by us in nothing."

Paul wounded them by confronting them with truth for the purpose of building them up, fostering them as a parent, rendering them as firm and faithful. He desired that they repent and turn their hearts to the Lord.

We have the command to speak the truth in love (Ephesians 4:15); we are to have the right spirit and attitude when speaking the truth. Yet, so often, the truth wounds, even when spoken in love. A true friend is one who risks wounding in order to speak truth; to hold that person accountable to the Word of God in order to build her up, support her, render her firm and faithful. That friend values your spiritual life even above the friendship because she wants you to seek the Lord and be right with Him.

If you have such a friend, thank God! May He give us the courage to be that friend. Not wounding for the purpose of hurting; but speaking the truth in love with the purpose of building, supporting, nurturing, and encouraging your friend to be firm and faithful to our precious Savior!

friendship

Notes

Prayers

Healthy or Unhealthy Friendships

By Renee Patton

Iron sharpeneth iron; so a man sharpeneth the countenance of his friend.

Proverbs 27:17

Have you ever had a really good friend? One with whom you did most everything? Talked to everyday? Sure, most of us have; yet are you truly satisfied with the friendship? Or does this friendship hurt or weigh you down? If the latter is your answer – you must act!

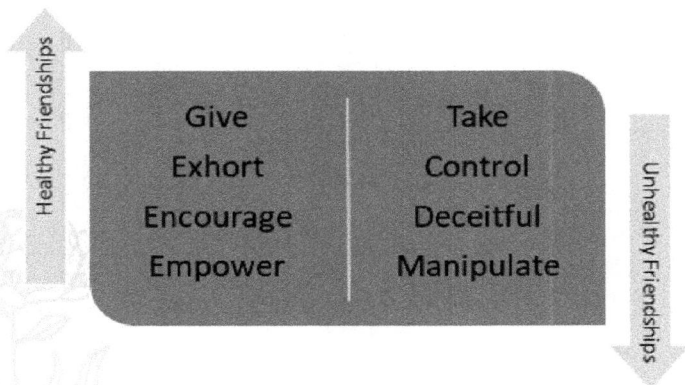

Healthy Friendships			Unhealthy Friendships
	Give	Take	
	Exhort	Control	
	Encourage	Deceitful	
	Empower	Manipulate	

Anyone can pick themselves up eventually; however, it is much easier to have the help of a friend to pick them up.

I believe the first place to start is with yourself! When I am faced with any unnerving situation, I try to scrutinize my perspective on friendship. Psalm 31:11, " I was a reproach among all mine enemies, but especially among my neighbours, and a fear to mine acquaintance: they that did see me without fled from me," is clear about others wanting to flee from the writer. If I am a reproach or make others fearful, I must first get myself right. I cannot be the one who uses my iron to hurt another!

Then ask yourself, "Does this person make me a better person" or "Do I make my friend a better person?" Proverbs 27:17 states, "Iron sharpeneth iron; so a man sharpeneth the countenance of his friend." So, does my friend sharpen me and do I sharpen them? Are we good for each other in that we exhort the other, encourage the other, and help the other to achieve their desires or goals? Or is it the contrary, controlling the friendship or manipulating or deceiving the other?

Additionally, a faithful friend will be there when we fall as in Ecclesiastes 4:9-10, "Two are better than one; because they have a good reward for their labour. For if they fall, the one will lift up his fellow: but woe to him that is alone when he falleth; for he hath not another to help him up." Anyone can pick themselves up eventually; however, it is much easier to have the help of a friend to pick them up. A healthy friendship gives to the other friend. Being there when needed provides encouragement and exhortation. One never knows just when another needs a helping hand, a prayer, or encouragement.

Finally, I may have to put distance between myself and a friend. Adding distance may bring tension. This will either bring you both closer or weed specific friends out. Because of the delicacy stepping back requires, remember not to let your mind be filled with the judgmental thoughts of others. These thoughts can quickly become out of control and take our minds down a wicked, destructive path! We must be diligent in "Casting down imaginations, and every high thing that exalteth itself against the knowledge of God, and bringing into captivity every thought to the obedience of Christ;" (II Corinthians 10:5).

These points I have had to come to myself. I had one particular friend, and we simply became too close. Soon she was dictating my schedule and voicing opinions about my other friendships. I had to step back and evaluate this particular friendship. Yes, I did have to tread delicate waters for a long while. However, God is so good! Through time and much prayer, we are friends today, yet not close. I do pray others never have to endure this; although if so, evaluate it and pray about it if such a time arises!

Do you periodically evaluate yourself and others in the friendships you have? Take action!

friendship

Notes

Prayers

The Blessing of Christian Friendship

By Marie Barron

---

*Fulfil ye my joy, that ye be likeminded, having the same love,
being of one accord, of one mind.*

Philippians 2:2

When I first started serving the Lord, I felt as if something was missing. I felt alone as I served. I needed someone who could share my blessings, concerns, and heartaches. I prayed and prayed for a Christian friend, someone who could understand me and help me along my journey. Proverbs 27:17, "Iron sharpeneth iron; so a man sharpeneth the countenance of his friend."

Six months later, God gave me a very special Christian friend! Proverbs 27:9, "Ointment and perfume rejoice the heart: so doth the sweetness of a man's friend by hearty counsel." It has been amazing to watch God cultivate and bless our friendship over the last forty-one years. At the time we met, we were young married ladies with children, struggling to grow and serve the Lord. We only lived two blocks from one another, therefore we were able to get together just about every day – such sweet fellowship.

Galatians 6:2, "Bear ye one another's burdens, and so fulfil the law of Christ." As time went on, I moved, and it became more difficult to get together, but we spoke on the phone all the time. We were able to see each other at church and still made a way to get together for special functions. Now this season of life has separated us even more due to health issues and just the busyness of life. However, it has not changed the closeness we share. It just makes the times we do get together even sweeter.

Proverbs 17:17a, "A friend loveth at all times...." Through the years God has given me many Christian friends, and I cherish each one of them. Philippians 1:3-5 says, "I thank my God upon every remembrance of you, Always in every prayer of mine for you all making request with joy, For your fellowship in the gospel from the first day until now." However, my very first Christian friend holds a very special place in my heart – forever friends!

For extra encouragement, look at Proverbs 18:24, "A man that hath friends must show himself friendly: and there is a friend that sticketh closer than a brother."

friendship

Notes

Prayers

A Thoughtful Friend

By Rachel Post

Withhold not good from them to whom it is due,
when it is in the power of thine hand to do it.

Proverbs 3:27

I have been guilty many times of having the intention to show myself friendly to someone and then not following through – whether out of forgetfulness, embarrassment, or some other reason. Maybe I noticed someone at church who seemed like they were struggling, or I was reminded of an old friend that I have not reached out to in awhile. I think to myself, "Hmm, I should pick up a gift card for that person or send an encouraging text message." And then, alas, I do neither of those things. The evening quickly approaches, and I am about to go to bed, and it hits me ... I never did send that text or pick up that little gift. Well, now it is too late in the day to be texting someone and all the stores are closed. "I will do it tomorrow," I think to myself as I crawl into bed. If we were taking bets, would you bet that I remembered to do it the following day? Nope, sure didn't.

We all know this story well, don't we? We are busy ladies and time is used getting the things done that "need" to be done. Maybe money is tight, and we shrug off helping someone because we simply "can't afford to." Trust me, I understand — we have all been there. But what if we took the mindset that helping people was something that "needed" to be done, and we could not afford not to. The Lord tells us not to withhold good when it is in the power of your hand to do it. I understand you may not be able to shake someone's hand at church and slip them a $100 bill, but you could possibly write an encouraging letter and even stick in a $10 Chick-Fil-A gift card (I know that would make my day). Do what you can to help encourage those that God has placed in your path. Allow the Spirit to lead you to that one person who could really use a friend today. Don't crawl into bed tonight with the regret of not being a thoughtful friend.

These little acts of kindness,
So easily out of mind,
These chances to be angels,
Which even mortals find—
They come in nights of silence,
To take away the grief,
When hope is faint and feeble,
And a drought has stopped belief.

It isn't the thing you do, dear,
It's the thing you leave undone,
That gives you the bitter heartache
At the setting of the sun;
The tender word unspoken,
The letter you did not write,
The flower you might have sent, dear,
Are your haunting ghosts at night.

For life is all too short, dear.
And sorrow is all too great,
To allow our slow compassion
That tarries until too late.
And it's not the thing you do, dear
It's the thing you leave undone,
That gives you the bitter heartache,
At the setting of the sun.

The stone you might have lifted
Out of your brother's way,
The bit of heartfelt counsel
You were hurried too much to say;
The loving touch of the hand, dear,
The gentle and winsome tone,
That you had no time or thought for,
With troubles enough of your own.

Poem By: Adelaide Procter

friendship

Notes

Prayers

True Friendship

By Hope Reimers

Create in me a clean heart, O God; and renew a right spirit within me.
Restore unto me the joy of thy salvation; and uphold me with thy free spirit.

Psalm 51:10,12

Throughout my life, I've had to fight envy toward sisters. As an only girl with two brothers, it was hard to relate to the sisterly things I'd hear, and I craved that type of relationship so much! They all had built-in best friends. There were seasons when I was blessed with friends I clicked with and seasons when it seemed like no one could really see or understand me. You may not actually relate to what I have to say at this point in your life, and that is completely okay! For those of you in a season of loneliness, I do have something to share that helped me greatly during some low points in my life.

I didn't realize how much I depended on friends until they weren't around anymore. I went on doing what I knew I was supposed to be doing, smiled on the outside, and served God to the best of my ability, but I found myself feeling like an empty shell. Many tears

As my Creator,
He knows me
well already,
but how much
do I know Him?

were shed, and I tried my best to hide them. My intuitive pastor's wife caught a glimpse of me during a moment of weakness and talked to me about it. I poured out everything I was thinking and feeling about the situation, and she was so understanding with her kind yet poignant words. It woke me up to the truth about myself.

I wanted a friendship with someone who could understand everything about me, think just like me, and understand exactly how I felt. What was completely wrong for me to do was to place that high expectation on any person when there's only One Who could fulfill that role. I realized I had a God-sized hole in my heart. That empty shell feeling was a result of placing people in a spot that only God could fill. I finally understood what losing the joy of your salvation meant. The lesson I learned was a strong reminder. It's one of the first spiritual lessons any Christian learns, and it is the fact that God needs to be the first priority in life. It's an extremely simple principle to learn, but we have a tendency to complicate things as life happens.

At that point in my life, I knew I had been closer to God before and was simply going through the motions of a Christian rather than maintaining the relationship I had with Him. Psalm 51:10,12 were the verses I needed to claim to get my spirit right with the Lord. "Create in me a clean heart, O God; and renew a right spirit within me. Restore unto me the joy of thy salvation; and uphold me with thy free spirit."

I learned that no one could ever understand me the way my Lord could. Jesus, above anyone else, knows what it's like to be lonely. Even among His closest friends, He saw that no one fully understood or agreed with His words or thoughts. He experienced what it was like to be completely alone on the cross when He was utterly forsaken. As my Creator, He knows me well already, but how much do I know Him? God craves the relationship we look for in other people. We know to listen to Him through His Word and preaching, but God also wants us to learn more about Him the same way we would try to get to know another person. We ask questions and opinions from other people. God desires us to connect with Him in the same way. True friendship is a choice found in Jesus Christ. What can you do now to strengthen your friendship with God?

friendship

Notes

Prayers

The Value of a Friend

By Sharon Garrett

Iron sharpeneth iron; so a man sharpeneth the countenance of his friend.

Proverbs 27:17

It is an interesting statement we find in this verse, "iron sharpeneth iron." Upon further investigation, I found that in days gone by, rubbing two pieces of iron together would restore the brilliance and sharpness of the iron. So, the two pieces of iron worked together to help each other. I love this example God uses in His Word to describe friendship.

I thank the Lord that I have had the blessing of a true friend for many years; as a matter of fact, over fifty years! Not all friendships last a lifetime, but I am very grateful for this friend God placed in my life. It all began in my home church during our teen years. She and I would get together and discuss our spiritual battles, our plans, our dreams, etc. in the light of God's Word. Because of the busyness of our lives, it was never hours at a time; but the precious part was when we could be together, we just picked up where we had left off. It was as though we were never apart. She moved out of state to go to college, and our correspondence continued. When she graduated, she was close by for a short while and moved away again to teach. We

85

faithfully wrote to each other although distance kept us physically apart. The joy of this friendship was that when I really needed some encouragement, her letter came, and it would be a blessing just when I needed it. The same happened with her. That is the friendship spoken of in Proverbs 27:17, "iron sharpeneth iron."

As the years passed, we married. We were now more settled in life. Then my husband and I went to the mission field. The distance that separated us was greater than ever. What would become of our friendship? The friendship continued. In our letters, we shared concerns for difficult situations; we assured each other of our prayers as we met challenges. We tried in every way to be a blessing to one another. Furlough times were a joy. We would almost run into each other's arms when we were reunited. We shared joys and sorrows, victories and battles, but we never tired of sharing our time together.

Circumstances beyond our control brought us back to the United States. Again, we were here but in different churches with different ministries, but we managed to stay in contact. Our friendship was not built on elaborate gifts nor frequent visits, but at every opportunity, we were talking and sharing. I always came away refreshed and encouraged.

Praise the Lord our friendship continues, and she is constantly a blessing in my life. This is a true "iron sharpeneth iron" friendship. I was reminded of I Samuel 23:16, "And Jonathan...went to David... and strengthened his hand in God." Are we the kind of friend that is a blessing?

friendship

Notes

Prayers

Ever Been Stepped On?
(When a Trusted Friend Betrays and Walks Away)

By Lydia L. Riley

Yea, mine own familiar friend, in whom I trusted,
which did eat of my bread, hath lifted up his heel against me.

Psalm 41:9

Psalm 55:12-14, "For it was not an enemy that reproached me; then I could have borne it: neither was it he that hated me that did magnify himself against me; then I would have hid myself from him: But it was thou, a man mine equal, my guide, and mine acquaintance. We took sweet counsel together, and walked unto the house of God in company."

Those who love deeply also hurt deeply. Jesus Himself experienced betrayal by a man whom He had accepted into His closest and most intimate circle. He called Judas "friend" in their parting words as He was betrayed with a kiss and abandoned in His darkest hours.

Sometimes, despite our greatest efforts for reconciliation, a person we love chooses to walk away. Betrayal by one whom you loved and deeply invested in can often take years to come to a semblance of healing. Because it is perceived as a "death" in our deepest emotions, we often experience all the steps of grief as we try to reconcile our inner turmoil and sense of loss.

89

What can we do as we try to pick up the pieces and work through the hurt and healing process? There is no simple "1-2-3" step process, but these truths can hopefully guide you to a place of renewed hope and vision.

Pour out your heart to the Lord. (Read the rest of Psalm 55 focusing on verses 1, 2, 16, 17, 22.) God is big enough. It's okay to "mourn in my complaint, and make a noise" — to "call upon God" and to come to Him throughout the day over and over (evening, morning, and noon) to pray and "cry aloud." "Cast thy burden upon the LORD, and he shall sustain thee..." He truly cares and listens to our cries; He is touched with the feeling of our infirmities!

Find hope in scriptures and promises. Stay in your Bible. The Lord can give you just what you need for "this day" from a Bible character or a precious personal nugget. Grab hold and don't let go of that Bible promise He gave to you, no matter how broken you might be feeling.

Seek counsel from trusted spiritual mentors. Having someone that listens and truly cares can make all the difference. Make sure to choose a Spirit-filled Christian who will always lovingly point you to Bible truths, while being a compassionate friend and voice of reason.

Realize that God sees the whole picture; there is good that can come from this. In future years, as life travels full circle, God might allow you to see the reason behind the suffering and betrayal. He did this for faithful Joseph in the Bible. He might also choose to never reveal the "why?" until eternity. You can trust Him. He can work all things for our good and His glory.

(Additional Resource for healing and dealing with injustice, discouragement, bitterness, severed relationships, and rejection: *When You Can't Just Get Over It: Biblical Insights for the Real World* by R.B. Ouellette.)

friendship

Notes

Prayers

To Have A Friend, Be A Friend

By Tricia Wood

A man that hath friends must shew himself friendly:
and there is a friend that sticketh closer than a brother.

Proverbs 18:24

God's Word is full of instructions about friendship, as well as many examples from which to learn. Each one gives us insight into different friendship relationships: David and Jonathan, Ruth and Naomi, Elijah and Elisha, Moses and Aaron, Elisabeth and Mary, and Paul and Timothy. The list could go on and on. Friendship relationships are very important and help encourage and strengthen us in our spiritual race.

How do I find such a friend? Proverbs 18:24 "A man that hath friends must shew himself friendly: and there is a friend that sticketh closer than a brother." This verse simply tells us that if we are to have a friend, we must be a friend. Although I cannot determine what kind of a friend one is to me, I can determine what kind of friend I will be to them.

While pondering these thoughts, I began to look at my dearest friends and what makes their friendship so special to me. I began to list qualities that I consider important to any friendship. The ones that quickly came to mind were truthfulness, trustworthiness, encouragement, supportiveness, godliness, thoughtfulness, and love. If these qualities are important to me in making a friendship great, then I must continually work on living these qualities myself so I can be a great friend.

Dale Carnegie said, "You can make more friends in two months by becoming interested in other people than you can in two years by trying to get other people interested in you." If you want a friend, be a friend. It really is that simple!

> Although I cannot determine what kind of a friend one is to me, I can determine what kind of friend I will be to them.

friendship

Notes

Prayers

A Friend of God

By Hannah Suttle

And the scripture was fulfilled which saith, Abraham believed God,
and it was imputed unto him for righteousness:
and he was called the Friend of God.

James 2:23

"Ye adulterers and adulteresses, know ye not that the friendship of the world is enmity with God? whosoever therefore will be a friend of the world is the enemy of God" (James 4:4). This verse is pretty straightforward in telling us that those who desire to be friends with the world cannot be the friend of God. Period. So besides being distinctly separate from the world, what more can I implement into my life? Throughout James 4, the Lord spoke to me about three simple things: submission, humility, and kindness.

"Submit yourselves therefore to God. Resist the devil, and he will flee from you" (James 4:7). As simple as it may sound, the first step in getting closer to the Lord is getting away from the devil! Submission means obedience not only to the Lord and His written Word but also to those who He has put in authority in our lives. Obedience and submission to authority, with a good attitude, puts a smile on the Lord's face!

97

"Humble yourselves in the sight of the Lord, and he shall lift you up" (James 4:10). There is nothing more elegant in my mind than a lady who knows her place and has a sweet and humble spirit about her. I wonder how much sweeter it is in the Lord's eyes? Many times, we do things in the ministry that seem to go unnoticed, but those with a humble spirit do not get discouraged about this! Serving with humility is not only working for the Lord but also directing all of the praise and honor back to Him.

"Speak not evil one of another, brethren" (James 4:11a). This is such a simple statement! Sarcasm and harsh words have quickly become a part of our culture, and many times we don't think twice about how our words can affect others deeply. Consistent kindness is something I've been working on recently and have started putting my words to this test: are my words kind, uplifting, and necessary? Let's not speak evil of one another. Instead, look for ways to lift each other!

The second definition of friend listed in the dictionary is "one who entertains for another sentiments of esteem, respect, and affection, which lead him to desire his company and seek to promote his happiness and prosperity." Imagine having that kind of relationship with the Lord: esteeming Him above all else; respecting Who He is as our Lord and Savior; loving Him with all your soul, mind, and strength; desiring to seek His company; promoting His happiness by seeking to please Him in all we do, say, and think; working to promote the prosperity of His gospel and church. What better friend to have than the Lord?

friendship

Notes

Prayers

Two Are Better Than One

By Judy Rolfe

*Two are better than one; because they have a good reward for their labour.
For if they fall, the one will lift up his fellow: but woe to him that is alone
when he falleth; for he hath not another to help him up.*

Ecclesiastes 4:9-10

I distinctly remember my very first friendship. It was when I entered Abner's Gap Elementary School as a first grader. It was a two-room schoolhouse with 1st-5th grades in one classroom. My friend's name was Patricia — which I thought was a beautiful name! She was in second grade. Soon after school began, I was promoted to second grade due to my mother preparing me for school at home. Kindergarten did not exist in the mountains of Virginia at that time.

Trish (which was her nickname) and I quickly became acquainted and remained best friends throughout elementary and high school. The two of us spent countless hours together and vowed that we would be friends forever. However, when graduation came, our lives went in opposite directions. Two years after graduation, when I was nineteen years old, I learned about salvation and accepted Jesus as my personal Savior. I reached out to tell her about this wonderful change in me, but she was not interested. Sadly, we are no longer friends.

101

Since that day, God has placed many special friends in my life. The first lady that I led to the Lord has been my faithful friend for over forty years. She and her husband are still serving the Lord today in Kansas. She is a strong Christian, and the two of us have spent countless hours fellowshipping together and talking about God's Word.

Another special friend shares my name – Judy! We met at a camp meeting in Elkton, MD. I was a new Christian, and she reached out to me and discipled me. The two of us went on visitation together which was a brand-new experience for me! She taught me the importance of reading my Bible and praying faithfully every day and setting my Christian standards high. Her friendship is priceless to me, and at eighty years of age, she is still serving the Lord and praying for me. Just as Judy inspired and motivated me, I want God to use my friendship with others in the same way.

Time and space do not permit me to mention the many others that have allowed me to be their friend, but I did save the one that is most special to me and has been my friend the longest as the last. This is my husband. The two of us have been married for almost fifty-three years! I cannot imagine where I would be today without his friendship. You see, he was the friend that took me to the church where I heard the Bible preached and learned about salvation. On August 29, 1971, he shared verses with me from Romans and Ephesians and knelt with me as I prayed and asked Jesus to be my Savior.

Amos 3:3 says, "How can two walk together except they be agreed?" I can only hope and pray that later in life Trish changed her mind and decided to become a Christian. I am so thankful for my many Christian friends because God is right – two are better than one!

friendship

Notes

Prayers

No Turning Back

By Christy Tadlock

Then said Jesus unto the twelve, Will ye also go away?
...we believe and are sure that thou art that Christ, the Son of the living God.

John 6:67, 69

John 6 is the longest chapter in the gospel of John and wow, does a lot take place. Things start off great! Jesus is being followed by a great multitude. His disciples are seeing and fellowshipping with the Son of God. They see Jesus feed the five thousand. They see Jesus walk on the sea. Things are going great.

Things get hard! Jesus speaks some complicated truths and doctrines to His followers and disciples. Many of the disciples even said, "... This is an hard saying; who can hear it?" (John 6:60). Many of his disciples got offended at what they heard. Things were hard.

Things get rough! After Jesus' hard saying "many of his disciples went back, and walked no more with him" (John 6:66). Because of the discourse given by Jesus, people became offended and left following Him. They just left. The Bible says they were "disciples," so they started off following Jesus. They were rubbing shoulders with Peter, James, and John. They were all friends and had fellowship one with another and with Christ. But they left. They stopped following.

105

They turned. So many "disciples" had left that Jesus even turned to His twelve disciples and said, "Will ye also go away?" Things were rough!

Things get real! Jesus questions the twelve disciples and asks if they will turn as well. Simon Peter steps up and answers, "... Lord, to whom shall we go? thou hast the words of eternal life. And we believe and are sure that thou are that Christ, the Son of the living God" (John 6:68-69). When faced with the question, "Will you leave also?" Peter undeniably spoke up – There is nowhere else to go. Nobody has what You have, Lord. Nobody can do what You do. Regardless of what others do, I am following You. I know and am sure that You are Jesus. I will follow on.

So let's apply this story in John 6 to real life and get to the point:

1. **Friends leave.** Friends leave the church. Friends leave Christ. Friends leave convictions. Many disciples left Jesus. Many disciples left Peter, James, John, and the others.

2. **Don't take it personally.** Don't take it personally. When some of the disciples left, they left Jesus because they were offended by His sayings. They left because they had a problem with God. It's not about you. When friends leave, they have a problem with Jesus, not you.

3. **Respond Biblically.** When others left, Peter didn't question. He didn't try to find out all the juicy details so he could sympathize. He simply resolved to continue. Don't let others leaving affect your faith and resolve.

106

friendship

Notes

Prayers

The Sweetness of Good Counsel Builds Friendships

By Marissa Patton

"Ointment and perfume rejoice the heart:
So doth the sweetness of a man's friend by hearty counsel."

Proverbs 27:9

During specific seasons of transition or uncertainty in my life, I have found older and wiser friends to help advise and encourage me. Here are a few things I have learned from these friendships along the way.

1. Ask for advice – Proverbs 3:13. Don't have too much pride to ask for help or feedback. Sometimes, we would rather try to figure it out for ourselves. I learned the hard way trial and error is often harder to endure than simply asking for help beforehand in marriage, ministry, motherhood, etc. I have found several invaluable sources of godly counsel. I have seen ladies who have walked my path and their "success" (through Christ). I desire the results that they have. It's hard to swallow pride and ask for help. But when I do, I often find that it leads to valuable wisdom ahead of time.

2. Listen and don't make excuses — Proverbs 2:1-5. Once I ask for advice, I must be willing to lay aside my bias and excuses. I have to truly listen to glean wisdom. It's easy to become defensive. It is far more difficult to be quiet and listen and take the constructive criticism that we sometimes need. I can't sit in denial. I can't become defensive. If I asked for counsel and someone was willing to share their thoughts with you, I must heed it!

3. Pray and be available — Proverbs 3:27. I need to be willing to listen or pray if my counselor friend is ever in need of my encouragement during a troubling time. If I see them in their struggle, I need to let them know that I am in their corner just as they were in mine! I can encourage and pray for them often.

You will be amazed at the benefits God brings through godly counsel! By seeking godly counsel, I have built some priceless friendships with "unlikely" ladies! Don't be afraid to ask for wise, godly counsel, be sure to heed the instruction given, and be available for them in their times of need.

It's hard to swallow pride and ask for help. But when I do, I often find that it leads to valuable wisdom ahead of time.

friendship

Notes

Prayers

Friendship Garden

By Sarah Russell

A man that hath friends must show himself friendly...

Proverbs 18:24

Who wants friends? If we're being honest, we all do! We want that sweet fellowship of friendship. Friendship is a part of God's design. The Bible speaks often of friendship. One of the most well-known verses on the topic of friendship is the verse above. In my life, the Lord has allowed me to have some wonderful friendships. But those friendships would have never begun and continued if we had not taken the time to cultivate and care for them.

Friendships must be cultivated like a garden. You must put forth the effort to have a rich, plentiful garden. First, you must start with the ground. Be sure the dirt is turned and ready for seeds. Just as you should prepare your heart for friendship, you need to be sure your heart is full of fresh, Christlike kindness and love.

Once our ground is ready, we must choose our seeds to plant. Friendships need to be based on more than common interests. True Christian friendship will be based on a mutual love for Christ.

A godly friend must be ready to warn, pray for, and challenge their friend.

(I would like to note that choosing friends based on their physical appearance is absolutely the wrong way to choose a friend. Being friends with beautiful people isn't wrong. But ignoring the "average-looking" person who has a heart to serve Jesus and others is most definitely wrong. Many friendships never began because of immature, surface judgment on a person's physical appearance.)

The next step is to carefully tend to our budding garden by watering and making sure it has enough sunlight. Shallow common interests will not aid in deepening the roots of friendship. It's going to take watering (the Word of God) and "Son" light. If our conversations never turn to the things of the Lord, we have a shallow-rooted friendship. A true, godly friendship must be rooted and grounded in Christ and the things of Christ.

When our friendship is rooted, then comes maintaining and enjoying the fruit! We must maintain our "Friendship Garden" by keeping out weeds of discord and bugs of bitterness. In my garden, some of my plants need pruning. Others need extra water and care to flourish and produce more fruit. Friendship is not only joy and laughter. At times, it is hard work and dedication. A godly friend must be ready to warn, pray for, and challenge their friend.

Read Proverbs 27:6 and 9. These verses speak of the faithful wounds of a friend and counsel by a friend. If you want a beautiful, flourishing friendship, you must be dedicated, caring, and ready to challenge your friends in Christ.

I believe Jesus is the supreme Friend and the true example of friendship. Jesus wisely chose His friends on earth. His disciples were all different. He may have shared similarities with some, and with others, He did not. He had many friends but only a few very close friendships. He was kind and caring but was not hesitant to lovingly point out wrong attitudes and behaviors. We would do well to study friendships throughout God's Word, but most of all, to pattern ourselves after Christ's example — the true Friend! I'm so thankful for the Friend we have in Jesus!

Challenge: Study the words friend, friends, and friendship in the book of Proverbs.

friendship

Notes

Prayers

What is a Real Friend?

By Kate Ledbetter

But I trust I shall shortly see thee, and we shall speak face to face. Peace be to thee. Our friends salute thee. Greet the friends by name.

III John 1:14

In the day and age we live in, many people don't seem to know what it is to be a real friend. Friendship has become very social media superficial. It's become empty promises and inability to communicate unless someone 100 percent agrees with you. No one is interested in being a friend that isn't invested in your life. No one is interested in having a friend that isn't the things listed below. Let's be determined to be genuine and real in how we conduct ourselves in friendship.

- A real friend is someone who speaks to you face to face. (Exodus 33:11)
- A real friend is someone who is there in your darkest hour. (Job 2:11)
- A real friend really loves you. (Proverbs 17:17)
- A real friend is friendly to you.(Proverbs 18:24a)

- A real friend sticks closer than a brother. (Proverbs 18:24b)
- A real friend will be faithful. The faithful friend may even hurt you with the truth. They will not be deceitful. (Proverbs 27:6)
- A real friend will give hearty, refreshing life in their counsel. They will make you feel alive. (Proverbs 27:9)
- A real friend helps knock the rough edges off of your life. (Proverbs 27:17)
- A real friend shares what Jesus has done in their life. (Mark 5:19)
- A real friend lays down their own life for their friend's - figuratively in their own selfishness and literally if life calls for it. (John 15:13)
- A real friend makes sure others know who their friends are. (III John 1:14)

Look through the list above and ask yourself what kind of friend you are. Do you have areas that need improvement? If so, why not give that to the Lord today and ask Him to turn you into a great friend!

friendship

Notes

Prayers

Jonathan:
An Example of Sacrificial Friendship

By Christina Weems

"Greater love hath no man than this, that a man lay down his life for his friends."

John 15:13

A true friend can be characterized by many qualities: caring, encouraging, helpful, honest, iron-sharpening, loving, loyal, kind, or truthful. However, one of the most outstanding characteristics of a real friendship is one's willingness to inconvenience himself for his friend. This term, known as sacrifice, is a Biblical command. We find it in Philippians 2:3, "... let each esteem other better than themselves." Someone who displays sacrifice resembles Christ, the greatest sacrificial Friend ever known. God's Word teaches us of such friendship in Jonathan, a man who put the needs of his friend before his own.

Jonathan's example is found in I Samuel 18. We are familiar with the strong bond of friendship between him and David, but do we really stop to think of all that he sacrificed for his friend? David was no kin to Jonathan, yet he loved him as his own soul (I Samuel 18:1). Just as his love was evident, so was his loyalty. Even though the king was actively trying to kill David, Jonathan was determined to stand by David's side. The king was none other than Saul, Jonathan's own father. No doubt this caused tension in their relationship as father and son, yet Jonathan's love and loyalty for David stood strong.

Lastly, the example of sacrificial friendship is given in the lengths Jonathan went to to protect David from harm. He even made a covenant with David (I Samuel 20:11-16), and when the situation proved necessary, he went the extra mile to protect the friend he loved so much (I Samuel 20:35-42). Jonathan showed by example that a true friend is willing to sacrifice everything to save those he loves.

John 15:13 says, "Greater love hath no man than this, that a man lay down his life for his friends." Jonathan's sacrificial friendship can be paralleled to the greatest example of Christ Himself, yet on a higher level. John 3:16 says, "For God so loved ... He gave ...." Christ manifested unfathomable love on Calvary's cross, yet he did not die for friends. He suffered for enemies, sinners, and those who hated Him. What a thought that the very people who shouted to crucify Him were the recipients of His sacrificial love. Christ also demonstrates loyalty to those who accept Him. Proverbs 18:24 says "... there is a friend that sticketh closer than a brother." Hebrews 13:5 promises, "I will never leave thee, nor forsake thee." Even though all friends may fail or forsake you, Christ promises to always walk by your side.

Lastly, Christ's great sacrifice proving His unending friendship and love was agonizing suffering and cruel death on the cross. His protection was sacrificing Himself to save us from eternal death. Thinking of our loving, loyal, and selfless Savior and Friend giving all, let these beautiful hymn lyrics resonate in your heart and mind — "What a friend we have in Jesus, all our sins and griefs to bear. What a privilege to carry everything to God in prayer."

friendship

Notes

Prayers

"Friendshipping" in the Hard Times

By Catherine Aylor

Faithful are the wounds of a friend; but the kisses of an enemy are deceitful. The full soul loatheth an honeycomb; but to the hungry soul every bitter thing is sweet. As a bird that wandereth from her nest, so is a man that wandereth from his place. Ointment and perfume rejoice the heart: so doth the sweetness of a man's friend by hearty counsel.

Proverbs 27:6-9

(Note: For those of you who know, I am a teacher. I do know that "friendshipping" is not a real word, but a great play on words for this thought today!)

Have you ever had a friend who is just your "BFF"? You do everything together. Maybe you have known them forever or maybe you met at a stage of life because of a unique situation or a difficult time in your life. Maybe they are a convenient friend because you just don't have anyone else you can really talk to.

Friendship is a beautiful thing. The Lord talked about friendship – read John 15:13-15 before continuing. But friendship, when used inappropriately, could be harmful. Sometimes in the hard times of

It may require
a good, godly friend to
put us in our place.
That doesn't always
feel good but is
sometimes necessary.

life, we can go to a friend (or a family member) more than we go to God because we want to recap or rehash the difficult times we are facing. In a human state of mind, we justify this as "seeking counsel" or fellowshipping. Often, this can be more damaging to our souls than we could imagine.

There are times we can go to friends for sweet counsel. I am not saying to stop doing this, but when "counsel sessions" turn into "gossip sessions," it is not beneficial to anyone. In Proverbs, it says, "Faithful are the wounds of a friend ...." In my life, I have been hurt by a friend (a term used lightly, more an acquaintance or someone you share casual conversation with). I also know I have probably been that friend who may have hurt another. I strive not to be or do this, but it can happen. I tend to talk to so many people. I do not have a lot of close friends, but I do have a lot of friends since I like to be friendly to anyone I meet.

I have been told on more than one occasion that I am easy to talk to. While it seems a good quality, it can also be a negative quality. When lending a listening ear or striving to help others grow in their spiritual walk as they are going through hard times, you may be the outlet they use to just vent rather than to seek a solution to the problem. Like the verse says, "... to the hungry soul every bitter thing is sweet." What this meant to me is if you are also going through a difficult time, you may do the same thing thinking you are helping each other. But you are both a stumbling block to the other in that bitter state of mind.

I feel more aware of this as I grow in the Lord and try to be preventative in these situations, but sometimes it can take a turn and end up going in the wrong direction. We need to be very mindful and always keep God at the center of our friendships and conversations. Being wounded or hurt by a friend can sometimes be a good thing. "What are you talking about? How could that possibly be a good thing!" Well, the truth of the matter is when we find ourselves talking about others, gossiping, venting, or sharing sorrow or trials frequently, it becomes detrimental to our conversations and spirit. It may require a good, godly friend to put us in our place. That doesn't always feel good but is sometimes necessary.

Those wounds are faithful because they are pointing us back to the John 15 Friend. You see He was and is a Friend that sticks closer than a brother (or sister). He gave such a good example of how we need to be a teacher, a servant, and a friend. He taught us that by laying down His life, it is not about us, but pointing others to a Saviour.

Sometimes people are unfair. Sometimes situations are tough. Sometimes those enemies give us deceitful kisses, making it seem like they are a friend. We feel betrayed. It is never right to treat our friendships as sounding boards to tell ourselves or others why we have been treated unfairly or unkindly. We should never make a case against others and their actions or justify ours in our friendships. We may have every right in our human perspective, but through the "... sweetness of a man's friend through hearty counsel" we can rejoice in our "friendshipping" in hard times. Know that godly counsel will strengthen us to not "... wander from our place" as the verse says and be a "perfume or ointment" type of friend rather than a stumbling block friend! Remember these words as we continue "friendshipping" with each other.

friendship

Notes

Prayers

The Only Friend You Really Need

By Grace Shiflett

Casting all your care upon him; for he careth for you.

I Peter 5:7

Has there ever been a time in your life where you felt like you didn't have a friend in the world? Maybe something happened and your friendship was shattered. Or you just felt like there was no one who would understand. Have you ever longed for that phone call or text message to reassure you there was a friend somewhere and the Lord had laid you on their heart? Maybe you felt you needed their prayers and needed to know they were praying for you? I don't know about you, but I have been there!

I remember a time in my life when the world around me seemed to crumble overnight. It was like a bad dream. What would I do now without those friends to support me? It was during that very low time in my life that I began to ask the Lord for help. My prayers were selfish at first. I only thought of myself in my pity party — desperate for friends who were no longer there. All the while, ignoring the One Who will never leave nor forsake us; the One that has promised to

133

hear us when we call. It was in those quiet days that the Lord taught me a valuable lesson about friendship. He wanted me to be content in knowing He was there, He cared, and He was enough. What more could I ask for than to know Jesus is my Friend? We have access anytime to draw nigh to God and be as close to Him as we want to be. This might sound childish to some, but oh what a wonderful day when I was content with only Him!

I cherish dear friendships greatly, but there are times when we go through things that we discover that His plan is for us to depend on Him and Him alone. At the time, it was not a fun lesson. But I look back, and I am so grateful that He drew me close to Him. He showed me how I had relied more on my friends than on Him. I desired their support and approval more than that of my heavenly Father. This lesson the Lord allowed me to learn many years ago changed my relationship with Him. It caused me to realize how much I had lived my life running to a friend or desiring a friend's support more than I ran to Him.

When the Lord takes you through places in life where you must walk alone, depending only on Him, you can truly know how important He is. The songwriter said it best;

What a Friend we have in Jesus,
All our sins and griefs to bear!
What a privilege to carry
Everything to God in prayer!
O what peace we often forfeit,
O what needless pain we bear,
All because we do not carry
Everything to God in prayer!

friendship

Notes

Prayers

Gift of Friendship:
Friends are a Gift from God

By Lois Van Zee

A man that hath friends must shew himself friendly:

Proverbs 18:24a

To have friends, we must show ourselves friendly. Here are just a few things that I thought about when I thought about what a friend truly is.

1. A friend is one who loveth at all times. Proverbs 17:17 says, "A friend loveth at all times, and a brother is born for adversity."

2. A friend is one who will rejoice with you. In the gospel of Luke, Luke shares with us how Mary went with haste to see Elisabeth. That is how it is when we enjoy the companionship of other women — we can't wait to share our good news and praises with them. These two women were first aligned with God and then with one another. These two women of faith truly left us an example of what Christian friendship should be about today.

3. A friend is one who must have compassion. The greatest example of this in the Bible is Jesus. In John 11:35, we find Jesus weeping over Lazarus' death when it says, "Jesus

137

wept." A friend is one who will pray for you. James 5:16 says, "Confess your faults one to another, and pray one for another, that ye may be healed. The effectual fervent prayer of a righteous man availeth much."

4. A friend is one who is honest when she knows you need to be rebuked. *Ouch*! We don't like that one, do we? But we all need friends who want the best for us even when it hurts. It says in Proverbs 27:5, "Open rebuke is better than secret love."

5. A friend is one who overlooks small things and does not get angry. Proverbs 19:11 says, "The discretion of a man deferreth his anger; and it is his glory to pass over a transgression." Be willing and ready to forgive a friend. Don't let things get in the way of a good friendship. Keep the ones you have. It has been said that you have many acquaintances but very few friends in life.

6. A friend is one who is trustworthy and faithful. We could say one who does not break confidence or one who won't talk or gossip behind your back. Proverbs 11:13 says, "A talebearer revealeth secrets: but he that is of a faithful spirit concealeth the matter." Let your friends know that you can be trusted. Then prove it to them by being a trustworthy and faithful friend.

I would like to leave you with this thought. It is good to be friends with one another, but it is even better to be God's friend. We find in James 2:23 where it says that Abraham was the friend of God. Abraham was the friend of God because he chose to believe in God and His Word, and we too can be a friend of God, if we choose to trust, obey, and believe Him and His Word.

friendship

Notes

Prayers

Two Are Better Than One

By Rhonda Simpson

Two are better than one; because they have a good reward for their labour.
For if they fall, the one will lift up his fellow: but woe to him that is alone
when he falleth; for he hath not another to help him up.

Ecclesiastes 4:9-10

Friendship is a precious commodity. No matter what age you are, young or old, true friends are so important. My life is made better because of the friends I have in my life. When I have something wonderful to share, I can't wait to tell my friend. When I have a heavy burden on my heart and feel like my world is crumbling, I need my friend's shoulder to cry on.

Scripture tells us that two are better than one. If one falls, they have another to lift them up. We all fall from time to time and what an encouragement it is to have a friend to pick us up. If you are alone, it's more tempting to stay in that fallen state. We need to choose friends that will help lift us up and tell us what we need to hear, not necessarily what we want to hear. A person left by themselves is in more danger of getting devoured by Satan. What you may not be

141

able to see even if it's right in front of you, your friend may be able to see and warn you about. We also need to be that kind of friend to others, that one who would encourage and lift up our friend and warn them if we see something troubling in their life.

Friendship should never be one-sided. I've had those kinds of "friends," and it is not encouraging. True friendship takes cultivating and work just as it would for a garden to grow. It has to be a give-and-take partnership. If you are always the taker or always the giver, that friendship won't last very long. That gets old quickly. Anything worth having takes work. As a friend, you also need to be a good listener. Be attentive and caring when your friend is talking to you. Their conversation is just as important as yours. For me, when you don't listen to what someone is saying, you are insinuating that what they are saying is not as important as what you are saying. Friendships are made stronger when you truly are a careful listener.

Ecclesiastes 4:9 says, "Two are better than one; because they have a good reward for their labour." The word good means "pleasure, precious, and sweet." The word reward means "benefit, wages, or worth." It is so rewarding and beneficial to have sweet, precious friends in your life. Choose them wisely. They will be the ones to help you up when you fall. Choose friends that will always be challenging you to be a better, stronger Christian. You both will be rewarded for this precious friendship.

friendship

Notes

Prayers

What a Friend We Have in Jesus

By Jana Buettner

I. Jesus is the Perfect Example of a Friend

WHAT A FRIEND WE HAVE IN JESUS

What a Friend we have in Jesus
All our sins and griefs to bear!
What a privilege to carry
Everything to God in prayer!
O what peace we often forfeit,
O what needless pain we bear,
All because we do not carry
Everything to God in prayer!

Have we trials and temptations?
Is there trouble anywhere?
We should never be discouraged,
Take it to the Lord in prayer.
Can we find a friend so faithful
Who will all our sorrows share?
Jesus knows our every weakness,
Take it to the Lord in prayer.

Are we weak and heavy laden,
Cumbered with a load of care? --
Precious Savior, still our refuge,
Take it to the Lord in prayer.
Do thy friends despise, forsake thee?
Take it to the Lord in prayer;
In His arms He'll take and shield thee,
Thou wilt find a solace there.

II. Jesus is the perfect example of what kind of a friend I should be.
   A. We're made in His image. (Romans 8:29b)
   B. We're made in His likeness. (Psalm 17:15b)
   C. Let Christ's mind be in yours. (Philippians 2:5)

III. What are His characteristics of being my Friend?
   A. He loves me and gave Himself for me.
      1. He loved me while I was a sinner and unlovely. (Romans 5:8, John 3:16-17)
      2. He loves His enemies. (Matthew 5:44, 46)
   B. He is no respecter of persons. (Romans 2:11)
   C. He is faithful to me. (Psalm 89:1; I John 1:9; Psalm 89:33)
   D. He is merciful to me. (Lamentations 3:21-24; Psalm 86:5; Psalm 86:13, 15)
   E. He forgives me. (Jeremiah 31:34b; Hebrews 10:17; Isaiah 43:25; Ephesians 4:32; Matthew 18:21, 22; Luke 17:3-4)
   F. He exhorts us.
      1. Our Purpose -- to walk with God. (Genesis 6:8, 9)
      2. Our Pattern -- to walk after Christ and please Him. (Hebrews 11:5; Colossians 2:6; Colossians 1:16b; Deuteronomy 6:5; I John 2:3, 6)
      3. Our Power -- to walk in the Spirit. (Galatians 5:16)
   G. He reproves and rebukes us. (Revelation 3:19; Proverbs 27:5-6; II Timothy 3:16-17; Hebrews 12:5-6; Colossians 1:22b,
   H. He prays and intercedes for us. (Hebrews 7:25b; John16-17)
   I. He comforts us. (II Corinthians 1:3, 4; Philippians 4:7; Isaiah 26:3)
   J. He is our hope and refuge. (Isaiah 41:10, 13; Deuteronomy 33:27; Isaiah 43:2; Psalm 86:7; Psalm 91:2-4, 15; Psalm 103:13, 14)

friendship

Notes

Prayers

About The Authors

Each author has been handpicked because of their testimony of Christ. God has gifted each writer with incredibly versatile perspectives of the Christian life. These godly ladies come from all walks of life including pastor's wives and daughters, missionary wives, church staff ladies, and faithful church members. Their written words of wisdom are sure to bless your heart.

To know more about our writers please visit:
thehighlyfavouredlife.com/our-story

Salvation Made Simple
By Renee Patton

Admit. One must first admit they are a sinner. Romans 3:10 states, "As it is written, There is none righteous, no, not one." Sin is everywhere and we all commit sin, many times without even trying. Perhaps in a conversation, we say something innocently, then realize it was not correct. That, my friend, is lying. Of course, murder is a sin that is seen and felt by those affected. However, lying is too. Jeremiah reminds one that "The heart is deceitful above all things, and desperately wicked: who can know it?" (17:9). A baby does not have to be told how to sin, it is simply in our nature. One must admit they are a sinner otherwise we make God a liar as found in I John 1:10, "If we say that we have not sinned, we make him a liar, and his word is not in us."

Believe. One must believe Jesus came to this earth to be born and die for our sins. "For God so loved the world, that he gave his only begotten Son, that whosoever believeth in him should not peish, but have everlasting life" (John 3:16). God desires that we should not perish, thus the choice is ours. God gives man the opportunity for salvation if man would take it. Romans 5:8 states "But God commendeth his love toward us, in that, while we were yet sinners, Christ died for us." Webster's 1828 Dictionary defines commendeth as entrusts or gives. So, God gave us His love through His Son, Jesus. Furthermore, Romans 5:19 shows how sin came from Adam and is made righteous through Christ, "For as by one man's disobedience [Adam] many were made sinners [mankind], so by the obedience of one [Jesus] shall many [mankind] be made righteous."

Confess. Confession is made with one's own mouth. The words must come from the person alone. Romans 10:9 talks of both confession and believing, "That if thou shalt confess with thy mouth the lord Jesus, and shalt believe in thine heart that God hath raised him from the dead, thou shalt be saved." The key is I have to confess to God. My husband or friend cannot confess for me. While God gives man the opportunity on earth, there will be a time every knee will bow and confess God is Lord, "For it is written, As I live, saith the Lord, every knee shall bow to me, and every tongue shall confess to God" (Romans 14:11).

To see more resources on salvation visit:
https://www.thehighlyfavouredlife.com/simple-salvation

If you made this decision, please contact us at *highlyfavouredlife @gmail.com*. We would love to rejoice with you in the new life you now have in Christ.

prayer

A Highly Favoured Life Devotional

Check Out
The Highly Favoured Life

on

and
thehighlyfavouredlife.com

www.ingramcontent.com/pod-product-compliance
Lightning Source LLC
Chambersburg PA
CBHW060323050426
42449CB00011B/2618